Brazil

A Picture Book for Young Explorers
Discover the Rich Geography, History, and Culture of Brazil

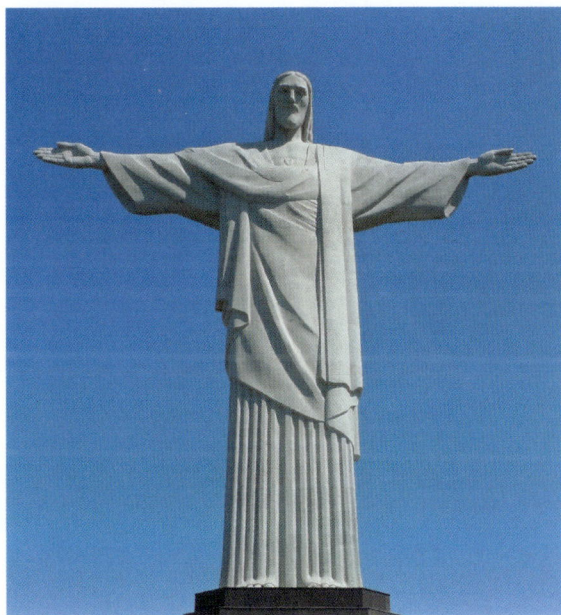

Visit our author page for more children's books
Amazon.com/author/88

By Nicole Damon

Introduction

Have you ever dreamed of visiting a place full of colorful birds, lush forests, incredible festivals, and fantastic soccer games? Welcome to Brazil! It's a huge country, the largest in South America, filled with adventure and wonder. Imagine standing at the edge of the mighty Amazon rainforest, home to playful monkeys and brightly colored parrots.

Sugarloaf Mountain (Pão de Açúcar)

Picture yourself dancing in the streets during Carnival, a giant festival filled with music, costumes, and smiles. In Brazil, you can also explore cities bursting with life, taste delicious foods, and meet friendly people who speak Portuguese. There's so much to discover in Brazil, from exciting wildlife to beautiful beaches. So grab your backpack, your curiosity, and get ready to explore this amazing country page by page!

Where in the World is Brazil?

Brazil is an enormous and exciting country located in the heart of South America. In fact, it's the largest country on the continent and the fifth largest on the planet! If you look at a world map, Brazil stands out like a giant puzzle piece, stretching from the warm tropical forests in the north all the way down to lush grasslands in the south. On its eastern side, Brazil meets the sparkling Atlantic Ocean, creating thousands of miles of breathtaking beaches filled with golden sand and turquoise waters.

Imagine building sandcastles, spotting dolphins, or simply splashing in the gentle waves. To the west, Brazil connects with other countries, making it a lively place full of diverse neighbors and cultures. This fantastic location means Brazil has many amazing landscapes—from sunny coastal towns to dense jungles, and even spectacular waterfalls. With so much variety, it's no wonder Brazil attracts explorers and adventurers from all around the world!

Brazil's landscape is incredibly diverse. In the north, you can find the famous Amazon rainforest, the biggest rainforest on Earth, home to millions of plants and animals. To the south, there are wide-open grasslands and impressive waterfalls like Iguazu Falls. Brazil even has mountains and savannahs! The capital city, Brasília, is located right in the middle of the country, designed in the shape of an airplane when viewed from above. Whether you're exploring cities, beaches, or wild jungles, Brazil's incredible geography offers endless adventures waiting for curious explorers like you!

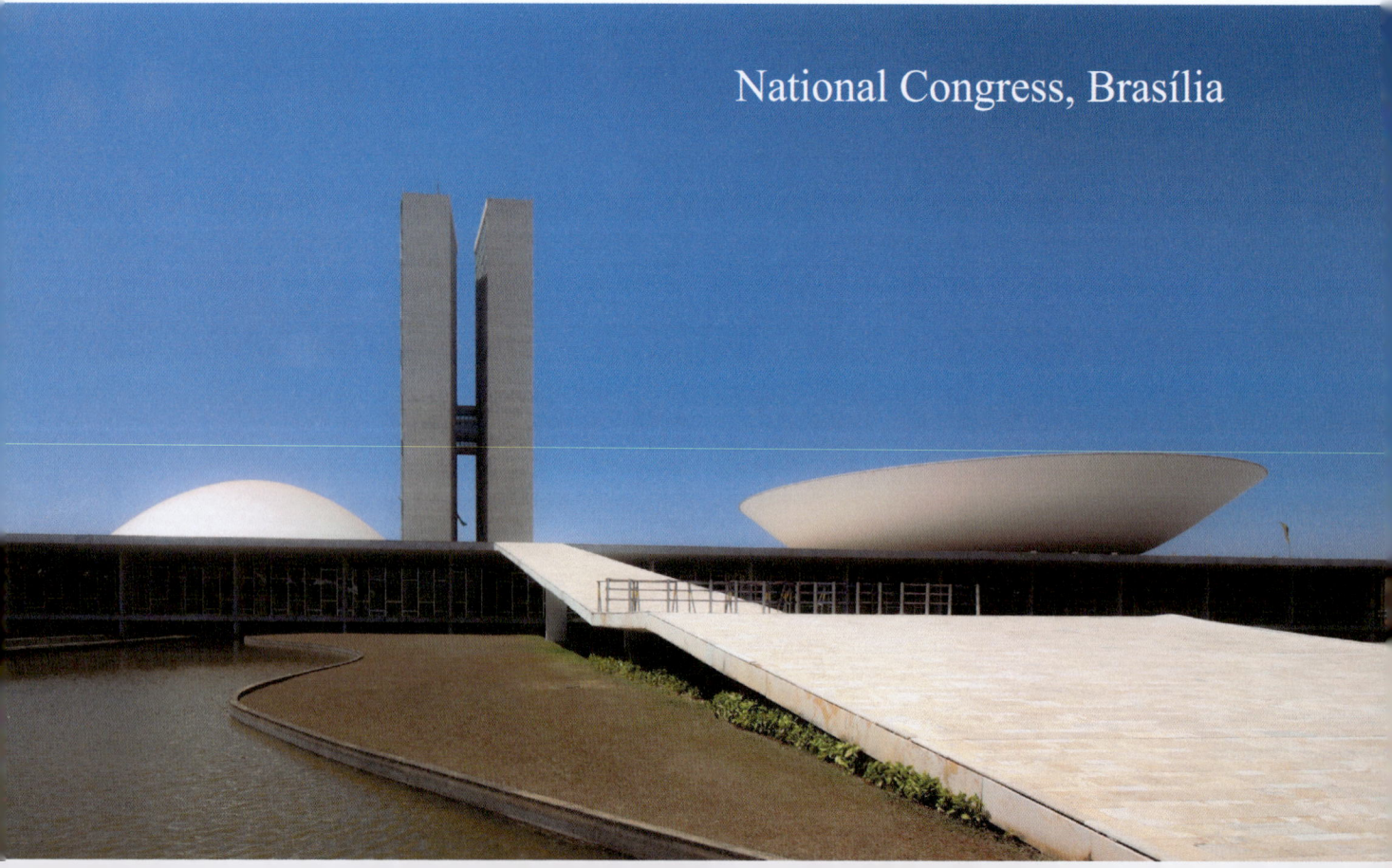

National Congress, Brasília

Journey Through History

Long before cities and skyscrapers dotted its landscape, Brazil was home to indigenous peoples who lived in harmony with nature. Hundreds of different tribes, such as the Tupi, Guarani, and Yanomami, inhabited Brazil's jungles, riversides, and grasslands. They built cozy villages, fished, hunted, and grew crops like corn and cassava. These early Brazilians had their own languages, traditions, and legends—many of which are still cherished today.

In the year 1500, Portuguese explorers arrived on the Brazilian coast. Led by Pedro Álvares Cabral, they claimed the land for Portugal. Soon, towns and farms started to appear. Brazil quickly became a colony, producing goods like sugar, coffee, and cotton. Sadly, this period brought great suffering, too, as millions of African people were forced into slavery and taken to Brazil. Their courage, strength, and resilience shaped Brazil's culture in many important ways, influencing music, food, dance, and religion.

In 1822, after many struggles, Brazil proudly declared independence from Portugal and became its own nation. The brave leader Dom Pedro I became Brazil's first emperor. Later, Brazil chose to become a republic, replacing the emperor with presidents chosen by its people.

Dom Pedro

Brazil's history includes heroes like Zumbi dos Palmares, who fought bravely against slavery, and famous inventors, explorers, and artists. Today, Brazilians celebrate their fascinating past through festivals, museums, and monuments. Understanding Brazil's journey through history helps us appreciate the rich traditions, joyful celebrations, and friendly spirit of the Brazilian people we meet today!

Brazil's Wonderful Culture

Brazil's culture is bursting with life, color, music, and joy! One of the most famous celebrations is Carnival, a giant festival filled with vibrant parades, fantastic costumes, and lively samba dancing. People from all over the world visit Brazil to join this exciting party, especially in cities like Rio de Janeiro and Salvador. Imagine streets filled with drumming, singing, and dazzling floats covered in feathers and glitter!

Music and dance are incredibly important in Brazil. Samba, a rhythmic and fast-paced dance, was created by blending African rhythms and local traditions. Brazilians also love soccer (called "futebol" in Portuguese), and it's a huge part of their daily lives. Kids and adults alike play soccer everywhere—from sandy beaches to city parks. Brazil has given the world legendary soccer players like Pelé, Ronaldo, and Neymar, who inspire millions.

Ronaldo Luís Nazário de Lima

Brazilian food is delicious and unique! You might enjoy feijoada, a tasty stew made with beans and meat, often served with rice and vegetables. Another yummy treat is brigadeiro, a chocolate sweet rolled in sprinkles—kids' favorite! Fresh fruit is everywhere, from juicy mangoes to sweet pineapples and bananas.

brigadeiro

The official language of Brazil is Portuguese, a language filled with beautiful sounds and expressions. Brazilians are friendly and welcoming, often greeting each other with smiles and hugs. Family and friends love spending time together, sharing stories, laughing, and enjoying music. Exploring Brazilian culture is a wonderful adventure—filled with fun traditions, mouth-watering food, and warm-hearted people who make visitors feel right at home!

Amazing Wildlife Wonders

Brazil is like a giant zoo without walls—it's home to more types of animals than almost any other country on Earth! The Amazon rainforest alone shelters millions of species, from tiny insects to enormous mammals. Imagine brightly colored parrots soaring through the treetops, playful monkeys swinging from branch to branch, and powerful jaguars quietly prowling beneath the thick jungle leaves.

One of Brazil's most famous creatures is the sloth, a slow-moving, tree-hugging animal that spends almost all its life hanging upside down in branches. And let's not forget about capybaras, the largest rodents in the world—friendly-looking animals that enjoy swimming in rivers and lakes. If you're lucky, you might spot a giant anteater, with its long snout specially designed for gobbling up ants!

Brazilian rivers and waters are filled with fascinating wildlife too. Pink river dolphins gracefully leap through the waters of the Amazon River, delighting visitors and locals alike. In the Pantanal wetlands, the world's largest tropical wetland, you can find caimans—cousins of crocodiles—sunbathing on the riverbanks, along with playful otters swimming nearby.

Bird lovers will be amazed by Brazil's feathered residents. Toucans, with their huge, colorful beaks, and macaws painted in brilliant blues, reds, and yellows, create breathtaking scenes in the sky. Even butterflies here come in every color you can imagine, dancing through the air like fluttering rainbows. Brazil's wildlife is incredible, unique, and precious—every animal playing a special role in this amazing country's natural wonders!

Best Places to Visit in Brazil

Brazil is filled with amazing places that adventurers dream about visiting! One of the most famous cities is **Rio de Janeiro**, known for its spectacular beaches like Copacabana and Ipanema. Here you can enjoy sunny days, build sandcastles, play beach soccer, or simply splash around in the waves. Don't miss the towering Christ the Redeemer statue, welcoming everyone with open arms from high above the city.

One of the coolest places to visit in Brazil is **Sugarloaf Mountain** in Rio de Janeiro! This giant, round-topped mountain rises high above the ocean and looks a little like a big loaf of sugar—hence its fun name. You can take a glass cable car all the way to the top, and the ride itself is an amazing adventure with stunning views! From the top, you can see the sparkling beaches, colorful city, and even little boats floating in the bay far below. It's the perfect spot to take pictures and feel like you're on top of the world!

High above the lively city of Rio de Janeiro stands **Christ the Redeemer**, one of the most famous statues in the world! This enormous statue of Jesus Christ spreads its arms wide open, as if welcoming everyone to Brazil with a friendly hug. Built nearly 100 years ago, it stands on Corcovado Mountain, offering incredible views of the city, beaches, and ocean far below. Made of strong concrete and covered in tiny pieces of soapstone, it shines beautifully in the sunlight. Millions of people visit every year, taking pictures and feeling amazed at how huge the statue really is—almost as tall as a 13-story building!

For nature lovers, the **Amazon rainforest** is an incredible destination. You can take a boat trip down the Amazon River, spotting pink dolphins, playful monkeys, and colorful birds. It's a real-life jungle adventure you'll never forget! Another breathtaking place is **Iguazu Falls**, one of the biggest waterfall systems in the world. Imagine standing near hundreds of powerful waterfalls crashing down, creating dazzling rainbows and clouds of mist. It's a truly magical sight.

Iguazu Falls

In the heart of Brazil is **Brasília**, the country's futuristic capital. Built in the shape of an airplane, Brasília is famous for its modern buildings, museums, and parks. Exploring this city feels like stepping into a sci-fi movie! And let's not forget the **Pantanal wetlands**, home to amazing wildlife. Here, you can spot jaguars, caimans, and capybaras up close, in their natural habitats.

Pantanal wetlands

Salvador, Brazil's first capital, preserves its history in the **architecture**, museums, and cultural landmarks scattered throughout. As you stroll through the **historic streets**, you'll discover stories from centuries ago, with many buildings restored to preserve the charm of the past. And don't miss trying **acarajé**, a deep-fried black-eyed pea dough filled with shrimp, representing Salvador's unique blend of African and Brazilian traditions. Whether through its music, food, or historic sights, Salvador offers an unforgettable cultural experience.

Everyday Life in Brazil

What's it like to be a kid in Brazil? It's full of fun, family, and friendship! Brazilian children enjoy playing outside with friends, especially soccer, the favorite sport. After school, parks, streets, and beaches quickly fill up with laughter as kids chase soccer balls and score goals.

School days in Brazil usually start early in the morning and end around lunchtime. Students learn Portuguese, math, science, geography, and history, just like you. After school, families often enjoy meals together. Rice, beans, meat, vegetables, and fresh fruit juice are popular choices, followed by tasty treats like brigadeiros or ice cream on special days.

Family is super important in Brazil. On weekends, Brazilians love to gather with cousins, grandparents, and neighbors. They have barbecues called "churrascos," play music, dance, and share stories. Birthdays are huge celebrations filled with cake, balloons, and lots of friends!

Many Brazilian kids also participate in special cultural events. During Carnival, they dress up in colorful costumes, dance samba, and watch spectacular parades. On Children's Day (October 12th), families celebrate by giving small gifts, having picnics, and going on fun trips together.

Life in Brazil is colorful and lively. Kids grow up surrounded by beautiful nature, exciting traditions, delicious food, and lots of music. Whether exploring local parks, joining festive celebrations, or just spending sunny afternoons with friends, Brazilian children live every day with joy and excitement, proud to share their wonderful country with others!

Protecting Brazil's Beautiful Nature

Brazil's forests, rivers, and animals are treasures worth protecting. But sadly, many of these wonderful places and creatures are in danger. Every year, parts of the Amazon rainforest are lost because of logging and farming. When trees disappear, animals lose their homes, rivers become polluted, and the Earth grows warmer.

Thankfully, Brazilians are stepping up to protect their beautiful country! People of all ages, including kids just like you, are joining together to help keep Brazil's nature safe. Across the country, communities plant new trees to help forests grow again. Scientists and volunteers rescue and care for injured animals, helping them return to the wild.

Brazilian schools teach kids the importance of recycling, saving water, and keeping parks and beaches clean. Young people create amazing projects to spread the word about saving nature, like art contests, music performances, and even special festivals.

Brazil's stunning wildlife and incredible forests belong to everyone. By working together, we can make sure that future generations get to see monkeys swinging through the trees, dolphins leaping in the rivers, and toucans soaring across the sky. Protecting Brazil's nature today means kids like you will have a greener, happier, and healthier planet to explore tomorrow!

Fun Facts About Brazil

Did you know Brazil has lots of cool secrets and fun surprises? Here are some amazing facts to impress your friends! First, Brazil is home to more than 211 million people, making it the largest country in South America by population! People in Brazil speak Portuguese—not Spanish like most of their neighbors. Brazil is the only country in South America that uses Portuguese as its official language.

Have you heard of the Amazon River? It's huge! In fact, the Amazon River is so long, powerful, and wide that in some places, you can't even see the other side! It holds more water than any other river in the world. Brazil also has the largest rainforest, the Amazon, where new animal species are discovered almost every day. Scientists think there are still many undiscovered creatures hidden deep in the jungle.

And here's a tasty fact: Brazil is the world's biggest coffee producer, growing more delicious coffee beans than any other country. Many adults around the world enjoy Brazilian coffee every morning. Soccer is a national passion! Brazil has won the FIFA World Cup more times than any other country—a total of five times! Many kids dream of becoming famous soccer players, just like their heroes.

Lastly, Brazil's flag features 27 stars representing its 26 states and one federal district. The flag's green color symbolizes the lush forests, and the yellow diamond represents gold resources. Brazil is full of surprises, adventures, and fascinating facts—there's always something new and exciting to discover about this amazing country!

Your Brazilian Adventure Awaits!

You've traveled across Brazil's incredible landscapes, danced through its vibrant culture, explored its amazing wildlife, and learned about its fascinating history. Brazil is truly a land filled with endless wonders and adventures waiting just for you.

Now it's your turn! Imagine yourself floating down the Amazon River, watching playful dolphins jump alongside your boat. Picture walking through colorful neighborhoods, tasting delicious Brazilian treats, and making new friends. Think about the music, laughter, and excitement you'll experience during Carnival celebrations or cheering loudly at a soccer game.

Remember, the world is big, and Brazil has taught us there's always something new to discover, explore, and cherish. Keep being curious, kind, and brave. Who knows? One day, your very own Brazilian adventure might begin! So pack your bags, grab your dreams, and get ready—the beauty and wonder of Brazil will be waiting for you!

Printed in Dunstable, United Kingdom